Presented To

_____

From

_____

Date

_____

A Soldiers Cookbook
1863

A Soldiers Cookbook 1863

Compiled by

Dean Drawbaugh

Copyright 2013 – Dean Drawbaugh
All rights reserved. This book is protected by the copyright laws of the United States of America. This book may not be copied or reprinted for commercial gain or profit. The use of short quotations or occasional page copying for personal use is permitted and encouraged. Permission will be granted upon request.
All rights reserved worldwide.
Drawbaugh Publishing Group
444 Allen Drive
Chambersburg PA 17202
ISBN 13: 978-0-9892680-1-1
For Worldwide Distribution, Printed in the United States.

1 2 3 4 5 6 7 8 9 10 / 17 16 15 14 13

Acknowledgments

I would like to recognize and thank G. Warren Elliott for his partnership on publishing this book. His drive and optimism are contagious.

Warren and I would like to thank all the soldiers that have sacrificed so much to allow this country to grow into a marvelous example of democracy for the world to see. May our soldiers' efforts never go unnoticed or be forgotten!

Table of Contents

Section I – Breads and Breakfast

Section II – Main Dishes

Section III – Vegetables

Section IV – Wild Game

Section V – Sweets and Treats

Foreword

A soldier's daily provisions

Meat:
- 12 ounces of pork or bacon, or 1 pound and 4 ounces of salt or fresh beef

Bread:
- 1 pound and 6 ounces of soft bread or flour, or 1 pound of hard bread [hardtack] or 1 pound and 4 ounces of cornmeal

To every 100 rations :
- 15 pounds of beans or peas, and
- 10 pounds of rice or hominy
- 10 pounds of green coffee, or 8 pounds of roasted and ground coffee or 1 pound and 8 ounces of tea
- 15 pounds of sugar
- 4 quarts of vinegar
- 3 pounds and 12 ounces of salt
- 4 ounces of pepper
- 30 pounds of potatoes when practical and
- 1 quart of molasses

The recipes in this soldier's cookbook use these supplies as a foundation to build the soldiers diet.

However soldiers of both armies needed to rely greatly on food sent from home, what they could hunt, or otherwise secure.

As other types of foods became available they adapted and incorporated them into a broader diet.

Section 1

Breads and Breakfast

Slapjacks

Take flour, little sugar and water, mix into paste, and fry the same as fritters in clean fat.

Sam's Marching Eggs

Eggs can be roasted by standing them on end in hot ashes. They will be boiled hard to carry in pocket on marches.

Indian Bread the major likes

One quart of buttermilk, one quart of cornmeal, one quart of flour, one cup of molasses, add a little soda and salt.

Eggs and Toasted Bread

3 large eggs
2 ounces butter
1 teaspoons cream or milk
Toasted bread

Mix eggs with butter, and milk. Heat the mix in a pan over fire keep stirring until it bubbles up, pour it on the toasted bread.

Hardtack

4 cups of flour
1-1/2 cups water
1 tablespoon of lard
1/2 teaspoon salt

Mix the flour, salt and water in a bowl. Adding the water gradually while stirring. Knead the dough in a bowl for 5 minutes. Let the mixture rest for 10 minutes then roll out to 1/2-inch thickness in a greased pan. Score into 3-inch sections and jab liberally with a fork. Bake at a medium heat for roughly 50-minutes. Break into pieces along scored lines and let cool.

Johnnie cakes

2 cups of cornmeal
2/3 cup of milk
2 tablespoons vegetable oil (lard)
1/2 teaspoon of salt

Mix all ingredients into a stiff batter and form eight biscuit-sized portions. Bake in a pan until brown.

Cornbread

1 tablespoons butter
2 cups white cornmeal
3/4 teaspoon salt
2 eggs
2 cups milk
1/4 cup oil

Mix the cornmeal, and salt in a large bowl. In another bowl whip the eggs with the milk and oil. Add the wet ingredients to the dry ingredients and stir until the dry ingredients are wet. Grease a pan and pour the batter into it. Bake 20-25 minutes or until the top is lightly browned.

Corn bread fritters

1 cup corn meal
1 cup flour
1/2 teaspoon salt
1 egg
Milk

Mix the dry ingredients together. Beat and egg with a little milk. Mix the dry ingredients with the wet ingredients. Add a good amount of lard to a hot pan so the fat is deeper then most frying. Drop mixture from a teaspoon into hot fat and cook until golden-brown.

Cornmeal pancakes

1 cup flour
1 teaspoon salt
1 cup corn meal
1 egg
1-3/4 cups milk
1/4 cup melted butter

Mix flour and salt. Add cornmeal and mix well. Add egg, milk and melted butter and mix until smooth. Melt lard in a hot pan spoon in mix and fry until golden-brown

Griddlecakes

2 eggs
2 cups flour
1-1/2 cups milk
2 teaspoons salt
1 tablespoon sugar
2 teaspoons melted butter

Mix the dry ingredients together then add the milk and eggs. Mix well and then add the melted butter. Fry in a hot greased pan.

Scones

2 cups flour
1/4 teaspoon salt
1 teaspoon sugar
1 egg
1 cup sour milk

Mix the dry ingredient and then combine with beaten egg and milk. Put on a floured board 1/2 inch thick and cut into small squares. Bake in a floured pan on low heat.

Cornmeal cakes

Cornmeal
Scalding water
Lard

Pour scalding water over salted cornmeal until moist allow the mixture to stand for an hour. Melt lard into a frying pan and scoop 3 teaspoons of mixture into the pan forming a cake 1/2 inch thick. When one side is done turn it over and brown the other side.

Section 2

Main Dishes

Joe's Easy Biscuits

One quart of sour milk, one teaspoonful of soda, one of salt, a piece of butter the half the size of a lemon, and flour enough to make them easy to roll out.

Leg of Pork

1 leg of pork
1/2 cup boiling water
Flour
Pepper
Salt
Vinegar

Score the skin in squares about half an inch. Place it in the pan with a little water. Heat slowly until you can see the fat coming out of the meat, then feed the fire to a red, steady glow. Spoon the water from the pan over the skin often, so it will not become tough. When the leg is done to your liking add seasoning like salt, pepper or vinegar to your liking.

You can also thicken the broth the pork was cooked in with a mixture of milk and flour to make gravy.

Roasted Chicken

Whole chicken
Butter
Browned flour

Place the chicken in the pan with a little water. Start by rubbing it with butter often until it is about half done. Continue cooking until you can turn the leg bone loose with your fingers. Season the remaining broth to taste and thicken with a mixture of milk and flour for gravy.

Fish Stew

Cod skull, sole, carp, trout, perch, eel or flounder
1/2 pint wine
1 quart beef broth, stock or consommé
1 large onion cut into small pieces
Pepper
Salt
Mushroom

Wash the fish, remove the bones, and cut into small pieces. Place the fish in the pot with other ingredients. Cover the kettle, and let it stew until the onions and mushrooms are tender.

Sausage & Apples

1 pound of sausage meat
3 large apples
1/2 cup brown sugar
Butter
Cinnamon

Fry sausage in a pan until just browned. Remove the sausage from the pan and pour off the fat. Melt enough butter to lightly cover the bottom of the pan. Slice apples to about 1/4 inch thick and place in pan over a low heat. When apples have softened slightly add a half-cup of brown sugar and a tablespoon of cinnamon. When the sugar and the butter form a thick syrup add the browned sausage and cook for another ten minutes or until done.

Chicken with Rice

1 chicken
Rice
Salt
Pepper

Place the chicken in a pot and cover it with water. Cover the pot and simmer for several hours until tender (add water if necessary). When the chicken is cooked remove bones, fat, and skin from chicken. Use the chicken broth to cook the rice; adding salt, pepper, and other spices to taste. Add chicken when rice is halfway done.

Navy Bean Soup

1 cup dried navy beans soaked for 12 hours
5 cups water
1/2 pound salt pork
2 large carrots chopped
1 large onion chopped
1 large potato, cut into 1/2 inch cubes
1 teaspoon salt
1/2 teaspoon pepper

Look over soaked beans and remove any discolored ones. Place the beans in a large pot add 5 cups water, salt pork, carrots and onions. Stir the mixture. Bring the soup to a boil, cover, and simmer 45 minutes or until the beans are tender. Add the potatoes and salt, and pepper to taste. Bring the soup to a boil, cover and cook until the potatoes are tender.

Hardtack Chowder

6 pieces hardtack
1-cup milk
1/4 pound salt pork cut into small cubes
1 large onion chopped
4 large potatoes, chopped
2 cups water
2 cups corn kernels
1 1/4 teaspoons salt

Soak the hardtack in milk until soft. Brown the salt pork in a pan then add onions and cook until soft. Then add potatoes and water and cook until potatoes are soft. Stir in hardtack, milk, and the remaining ingredients. Stir often while heating and serve when it's almost ready to boil.

Cornmeal Dumplings

1 cup cornmeal
1-1/2 cups of boiling water
3 tablespoons of pork drippings
1/2 teaspoon salt

Mix cornmeal, water, and drippings make into a stiff dough. Shape into dumplings about 2 inches long and 1/2 inch thick. Place on top of a boiling stew. Cover the pan and cook slowly for 10 minutes. Turn over and cook for another 10 minutes or until firm.

Salt Pork and Gravy

1 pound of salt pork
1 cup flour
Milk
Salt
Pepper

Start with a thin slices of salt pork. Dip each into the flour on both sides and fry in a greased pan until golden-brown. Drain most of the grease, add two to three tablespoons of flour to the pan and let cook a couple of minutes to let the fat mix with the flour. Remove the pan from the fire and add the milk in slowly while continuing to stir. Pour over the salt pork.

Salt Pork and Fried Potatoes

1 pound salt pork
2-cups boiled potatoes sliced thin
Salt
Pepper

Fry the salt pork in a hot pan. There should be a fair amount of fat left in the pan. Mix the sliced potatoes with the fat and add salt and pepper. Fry the mixture stirring constantly until well browned.

Chicken fried steak

1 round steak cut ¾ inch thick
Salt
Pepper
Flour
Lard

Rub steak with salt and pepper. Pound all the flour possible into steak. Melt lard in a pan and sear the steak on both sides. Cook until brown.

Liver and Bacon

1 pound of liver sliced to 1/2 inch thick
12 slices of bacon
1 large onion sliced
Salt
Pepper

Wash liver and add to boiling water that covers the liver cook for 5 minutes then drain. Brown bacon in a hot pan then add liver. Cook, turning often for about 5 minutes. Add sliced onion. Cook until onions and liver are browned but liver is not dry.

Pan-fried chicken

1 chicken cut in pieces
Salt
Pepper
Flour
Lard

Rub chicken with salt and pepper then roll in the flour. Melt lard into a frying pan and brown the chicken in the hot fat. Cover the pan and cook over low heat until tender.

Sausage and Vegetables

1 pound of sausage in patties
1 onion
4 potatoes
2 turnips
2 carrots
1 cup of tomatoes

Lay the sausage in the middle of a frying pan and slice the vegetables around the sausage. Add a little water. When the sausage begins to cook, break it in pieces with a fork. Add the tomatoes and season to taste.

Fish Cakes

Any fish will do!
2 cups cold broiled fish flaked
2 cups mashed potatoes
1 tablespoon butter
1 beaten egg
Salt
Pepper

Mix all ingredients together and shape into round flat cakes 1/2 inch thick. Coat both sides with flour and fry in lard until hot in the middle.

Chicken Stoltzfus

5 pounds chicken pieces
1 1/2 quarts of water
1 tablespoon salt
Pepper
3/8 pound of butter
1/2 cup flour
1 cup light cream
Parsley chopped

Place chicken pieces in large pot and cover with water. Add salt and pepper and bring to a boil. Simmer, partially covered for 1-hour. Remove chicken, cool, and remove bone. Cut into bite-sized pieces. Strain stock, return to pan, and simmer until reduced to four cups. Pour stock into bowl and reserve. In the same pot stock melt butter. Mix in flour and cook over medium low heat until golden and bubbly. Add the 4 cups chicken stock and the cream, stirring constantly. Cook on medium high until the sauce boils, then simmer until thick and smooth. Add the chicken and parsley.

Pastry squares for Chicken Stoltzfus

1/2 cup lard
1/2 cup butter
1 teaspoon salt
3 cups flour
1/2 cup cold water

Mix the lard and butter into the flour. Sprinkle with cold water and toss lightly. Use only enough water to hold the dough together. Press dough into a ball and place on a lightly floured surface. Divide into 3 parts. Roll each part 1/8 inch thick. Put in pan and with a sharp knife, cut dough into one-inch squares. Bake on medium heat for 12 to 15 minutes until lightly browned. Spoon the chicken mixture over-the-top and serve.

Section 3

Vegetables

Corn on the Cob

Boil water and add the corn still on the cob. Cook until tender. Eat plain or with butter or salt.

Pumpkin Bread from Robert

Peel a small pumpkin remove the seeds and cut it in to small pieces. Boil the pieces in water till they becomes thick, remove as much water as possible, and mix flour to make good dough. Bake into a bread

Baked Potato – put on ashes

Select medium sized potatoes with a smooth skin and wash thoroughly. Bake at high heat for 40-60 minutes.

Potato Cakes

6 potatoes
Butter
Water

Boil six good-sized potatoes, and mash them fine, add salt, a spoonful of butter, and two cups of water, while they are hot, then work in flour enough for making a very thick paste. Fry them like you would a pancake.

Fried Cucumbers

Cucumbers skinned and cut into 1/4 inch slices
Bread crumbs

Dip the slices in water and then into the breadcrumbs. Fry until golden-brown in a pan after ham or salt pork to pick up the flavor.

Lettuce Dressing

1/2 cup sugar
1/4 cup vinegar
1/2 teaspoon salt
2 eggs

Mix all ingredients well and pour over lettuce for a great salad.

Fried Green Tomatoes

2 green tomatoes sliced about 1/8 inch thick
Flour
Salt
Pepper

After frying ham, pork or other meat, dip the tomato slices in water and then flour on both sides. Fry the tomatoes until golden-brown. Season tomatoes with salt and pepper to taste.

Sweet Potatoes

3 cups of sweet potatoes in 1/2 inch cubes
1 tablespoon of butter
3 tablespoons of molasses.
1/4 cup of water

Place all in a pan and cook on low heat until the sweet potatoes are soft. Add more water if necessary.

Baked Corn

2 cups of corn
2 eggs well beaten
1 tablespoon butter
2 teaspoons flour
2 tablespoons milk
2 tablespoons cream
1 teaspoon salt

Combine all ingredients and mix thoroughly. Pour the mixture into a well-oiled pan and set the pan in warm water. Bake in moderate heat until an inserted knife comes out clean.

Potato Hash

4 to 6 potatoes
2 cups of diced meat
2 tablespoons celery chopped
1 tablespoon green pepper chopped
1 medium-sized onion chopped
Lard

Melt lard in a hot frying pan add the celery, green pepper, and onion and cook until slightly tender. Add the raw potatoes and cook until slightly brown. Add meat and season to taste. Keep over a slow flame for about 12 to 20 minutes stirring occasionally.

Cooked Red Cabbage

1 head of red cabbage shredded
1 large apple sliced
8 tablespoons vinegar
3 tablespoons of sugar, salt, pepper
1 tablespoon lard
1 tablespoon butter

Add the shredded cabbage to the other ingredients and cook. Add water if necessary but you should have enough water from the cabbage.

Apple-sweet potato casserole

3 cups sliced sweet potatoes
2 cups sliced tart apples
8 strips crisp fried bacon
Salt
Sugar
Butter

Layer ingredients in a greased pan, seasoning each layer with salt, sugar and butter. Bake one hour on low to medium heat.

Corn Fritters

2 cups corn
2 teaspoons salt
2 cups flour
2 eggs
Lard

Mix corn, salt, flour, and eggs together until an even mix. Melt lard in bottom of pan and fry the mix like a pancake.

Section 4

Wild game

Barley Water – try this at home

Put into a jug one ounce of pearl barley, half an ounce of white sugar and the rind of a lemon. Add one quart of boiling water, and let it stand for eight or ten hours then strain off the liquor.

Venison Pot Roast

4 pound of venison
1/2 cup of flour
2 tablespoons of vinegar
Salt
Pepper

Mix the salt, pepper and flour and rub into the meat. Brown in a hot fat and then put into a pot for cooking adding the vinegar and water as needed. Cover and cook for 2 hours at medium heat.

Turtle soup

2 pounds of diced turtle meat
1 cup water
1 cup wine
1 chopped onion
2 tablespoons of butter
1 tablespoon flour

Cook onion in butter, slowly add in the flour. Add the remaining ingredient and cook on a low heat for 30 minutes.

Trout

2 pounds of trout
1/2 cup chopped onions
6 tablespoons melted butter
1/4 teaspoon salt

Heat the onion in butter then add the salt. Put in a greased pan and make shallow cuts on the top. Bake uncovered over medium heat for 10 minutes spooning melted butter over the trout until brown on all sides. Almost cover the trout with boiling water and simmer until meat is tender.

Roast Grouse

4 grouse
4 tablespoons of butter
8 slices of bacon
Salt
Pepper
Apple or Onion

Clean bird and salt and pepper both inside and out. Stuff with apples or onions add one tablespoon of butter to each body cavity. Cover breasts with bacon slices and roast uncovered on medium heat for 30 minutes. Discard apples or onions as these were used to remove the gamy taste from the meat.

Fried Rabbit

1 rabbit
1 cup flour
1/4 teaspoon pepper
1 teaspoon salt
1 chopped onion
4 tablespoons of lard
1 teaspoon vinegar

Mix the flour, salt and pepper. Cut the rabbit into serving size; dip in the mixture of flour, salt, and pepper. Melt lard into a pan and brown the rabbit, then add a small amount of water, onions, and vinegar. Cook on low heat until tender.

Crawdads

2-3 quarts water
Juice from 1 lemon
1 small onion, chopped
1 stalk celery with leaves, chopped
1 clove garlic, chopped
2-3 dozen crawdads

Twist off the tail and discard the upper body of crawdad. Combine water, lemon juice, onion, celery and garlic in pot and heat to boiling. Add crawdads and heat pot until the water is boiling again, then back off heat and wait until meat is opaque (white) all the way through. Remove from the pot or it will overcook.

Venison chops

Venison chops or steaks
Lard
1 onion chopped
Salt
Pepper

Melt lard in a frying pan and sauté onions in the fat. Score the edges of the meat to prevent them from curling. Use the salt and pepper as a rub for the surface of the meat. Add the meat to the pan and fry until brown, and then cook slowly until tender.

Groundhog

1 young groundhog skinned and cleaned
1/2 cup flour
1/4 teaspoon flour
1/4 teaspoon salt
6 teaspoons shortening
1 teaspoon sugar
1/2 cup warm water

Cut the meat into serving pieces and soak the groundhog in saltwater overnight. Mix the flour, salt, and pepper and rub into the meat. Melt lard into a frying pan and brown the meat. Sprinkle the meat with sugar and add water. Cover the pan and let simmer for 40 minutes or until tender. Cover can be removed 15 minutes before its done to allow it to brown.

Section 5

Sweets and Treats

Rice Pudding

Take one cup of soft-boiled rice, a pint of milk, a cup of sugar, three eggs, and a piece of butter the size of a walnut. Cook

Acorn Coffee - not bad

Take ripe acorns, wash them while in the shell, dry them, and fry in a pan until they pop open. Remove the shell and roast with a little bacon fat. Add water for a cup of coffee.

Egg Pudding

4 large eggs
4 cups of milk
4 tablespoons of flour
4 tablespoons of sugar
Salt
Butter

Mix eggs, milk and a little salt, stir in four large spoonfuls of flour, and sugar to your taste. Pour into small cups that have been greased with butter, filling them a bit more than half-full. Bake for fifteen minutes.

Baked Apples

5 apples – cored and sliced into narrow wedges
4 tablespoons butter
1 cup brown sugar
1/2 teaspoon nutmeg or cinnamon

Melt the butter in a pan and add the apples. Cover the skillet and cook the apples 5 minutes over a low heat. Add the brown sugar and the nutmeg. Stir the mixture well. Cook the apples for 10-12 minutes or until tender, checking every few minutes. Add water if needed to prevent the apples from sticking to the pan.

Corn Pudding

1 pint grated corn
1 tablespoon flour
2 tablespoons melted butter
2 tablespoons sugar
1 teaspoon salt
1/4 teaspoon pepper
3 eggs beaten
1 cup milk

Mix flour, sugar, salt, pepper, melted butter, and eggs mix well and add milk, bake at medium heat for 45 minutes.

Fried Apples

2-3 apples – cored and cut into 1/2 inch slices
Sugar or cinnamon
Lard

Fry in hot lard until tender and glazed on both sides. Sprinkle with sugar or cinnamon.

Apple Sauce

6 tart apples
2/3 cup sugar
1 cup water

Wash, core apples, and cut into quarters. Put apples, sugar, and water into a pan and cook slowly until apples are very soft. Mash the apples as fine as possible.

Bread pudding

4 slices buttered bread cut in squares
1/2 cup sugar
3 eggs
1 cup milk

Mix eggs, sugar, and milk in a small pan. Add the buttered bread and bake on low heat for about 40 minutes or until custard is set.

Potato Candy

1/2 dozen small white potatoes, peeled
1 plus lbs powdered sugar
1 Tbsp vanilla
1pound peanut butter

Cook peeled potatoes in lightly salted water. When soft, drain and mash. Add powdered sugar gradually and stir until stiff. Add vanilla. Roll dough out flat and spread the peanut butter on it. Place it on ice. When well chilled, slice and serve.

www.ingramcontent.com/pod-product-compliance
Lightning Source LLC
Chambersburg PA
CBHW032104040426
42449CB00007B/1179